Treas

Spanish Love

More *Treasury of Love*

Treasury of Arabic Love

Treasury of Finnish Love

Treasury of French Love

Treasury of German Love

Treasury of Italian Love

Treasury of Jewish Love

Treasury of Polish Love

Treasury of Roman Love

Treasury of Russian Love

Each collection is also available as an Audio Book.

HIPPOCRENE BOOKS
171 Madison Avenue
New York, NY 10016

Treasury of
Spanish Love

Poems, Quotations and Proverbs

In Spanish and English

Edited and Translated by

Juan and Susan Serrano

HIPPOCRENE BOOKS
New York

All translations by Juan and Susan Serrano, editors, except those on the following pages: 14-15, 20-21, 32-33, 34-37, 42-43, 44-45, 46-47, 52-53, 54-55, 56-57, 58-59, 60-61, 80-81. See page 128 for additional information.

Contents
Spanish Love Poems

Spanish Love Quotations and Proverbs
follow page 96

Spanish Love Poems

Jarchas (11th-13th centuries)

Tanto amar

Tanto amar, tanto amar,
amigo, tanto amar.
Enfermaron mis ojos alegres
y duelen tan mal.

Yosef-al-Katib

Señor mío Ibrahim

Señor mío Ibrahim,
oh nombre dulce,
vente a mí
de noche.
Si no, si no quieres,
iréme a ti.
Dime en dónde
encontrarte.

Muhammad ibn Ubada

Sí. ¡Ay, mi señor!

Sí. ¡Ay, mi señor!
Que no beses
mi boquita roja.
Seré como el azafrán.

'Ubada

Jarchas

Jarchas are the earliest poems written in Spanish. They were written by Arabic and Hebrew poets in Islamic Spain between 11th and 13th centuries. The jarcha is a short refrain, or last stanza of a song, in which a love-struck girl speaks to her mother or friends about her passion and sorrow. Her lover (*habib*) is usually referred to as 'friend.' The first European lyric known in a modern Romance language is the jarcha by the Jewish poet Yosef al-Katib (Scriba) c. 1042. By their very nature, these primitive poems are very simple, and it is their simplicity which makes them so beautiful and moving.

So much love

So much love, so much love,
My friend, so much love,
My happy eyes are infirmed
And the pain is so bad.

My Lord Ibrahim

My Lord Ibrahim,
Oh name most sweet,
Come to me
By night.
If not, if thou dost detain,
I shall go to thee.
Tell me where
Thou shalt be.

Yes, Oh my lord

Yes, Oh my lord,
Do not kiss
My red lips,
For I shall turn to saffron.

Di, si eres adivina

Di, si eres adivina
y adivinas en verdad,
dime cuándo me vendrá
mi amado Isaac.

Yehuda Halevi

Se va mi corazón de mí

Se va mi corazón de mí.
¡Oh Señor! ¿me tornará?
¡Tan malo es mi dolor por el amigo!
Está enfermo. ¿Cuándo sanará?

Yehuda Halevi

Boquita de perlas

Boquita de perlas
dulce como la miel,
vente, bésame,
amado, vente a mí.

Al-Sairafi

Si me quieres

Si me quieres como bueno,
bésame esta sarta de perlas,
¡boquita de cerezas!

Anonymous

Tell me, if you are a diviner

Tell me, if you are a diviner
And divine you truly can,
Tell me when he'll come back
My beloved Isaac.

My heart is leaving me

My heart is leaving me,
Oh Lord, will it come back again?
So strong is this ache for my love!
He's ill—will he his strength regain?

Little mouth of pearls

Little mouth of pearls,
Sweet as honey true,
Come, kiss me
My love, come to me, do.

If thou desirest me

If thou desirest me as a tasty morsel,
Kiss this my string of pearls,
Little mouth of cherries!

Arcipreste de Hita (1283-1350)

Doña Endrina

¡Ay, cuán hermosa viene doña Endrina por la plaza!
¡Qué talle, qué donaire, qué alto cuello de garza!
¡Qué cabellos, qué boquilla, qué color, qué buenandanza!
Con saetas de amor hiere, cuando los sus ojos alza.

. . . . .

En el mundo no es cosa que yo ame a par de vos;
tiempo es ya pasado, de los años más de dos,
que por vuestro amor me pena: ámoos más que a Dios.
No oso poner persona que lo hable entre nos.

Con la gran pena que paso, véngoos decir mi queja:
vuestro amor y deseo que me ahinca y me aqueja,
no me tira, no me parte, no me suelta, no me deja:
tanto me da la muerte, cuanto más se me aleja.

. . . . .

Doña Endrina

Ah, what a picture's Doña Endrina walking through the
    square!
What a figure, what graceful mien, what swanlike neck so fair,
Such lustrous hair, little mouth, such colour and poise most
    rare.
Arrows of love pierce my heart when her eyes release their
    flare.

. . . . .

In this world, Oh sweet desire, I love no-one above you;
Time has sped past, an eternity, though in years but two,
That for your love I pine: I love you more than God 'tis true.
I dare not ask some go-between with you my case pursue.

In great woe I come before you to give my lament rein,
This love and desire pierce so deep, I'm left in throbbing pain,
It will not go, will not leave me, will not release the strain:
The more love retreats, the more I die, this I do not feign.

. . . . .

Amor

El amor haz sutil al hombre que es rudo,
hácele hablar hermoso al que antes es mudo,
al hombre que es cobarde hácelo muy atrevudo,
al perezoso hace ser presto y agudo.

Al mancebo mantiene mucho en mancebez,
y al viejo haz perder mucho la vejez,
hace blanco y hermoso del negro como pez,
lo que no vale una nuez amor le da gran prez.

. . . .

De las propiedades que las dueñas chicas han

En pequeña girgonza yace gran resplandor,
en azúcar muy poco yace mucho dulzor,
en la dueña pequeña yace muy gran amor,
pocas palabras cumplen al buen entendedor.

Es pequeño el grano de la buena pimienta,
pero más que la nuez conforta y calienta,
así dueña pequeña, si todo amor consienta,
no hay placer del mundo que en ella no sienta.

Como en chica rosa está mucha color,
y en oro muy poco gran precio y gran valor,
como un poco bálsamo yace gran buen olor,
así en dueña chica yace muy gran sabor.

Love

Love to the slowest subtilty can teach,
And to the dumb give fair and flowing speech,
It makes the coward daring, and the dull
And idle diligent and promptness-full.

It makes youth ever youthful; takes from age
The heavy burden of time's pilgrimage;
Gives beauty to deformity; it seem
To value what is valueless and mean.

. . . .

Praise of Little Women

In a little precious stone what splendor meets the eyes!
In a little lump of sugar how much of sweetness lies!
So in a little woman love grows and multiplies;
You recollect the proverb says,—'a word unto the Wise.'

A pepper-corn is very small, but seasons every dinner
More than all other condiments, although 'tis sprinkled
    thinner;
Just so a little woman is, if Love will let you win her.
There's not a joy in all the world you will not find within her.

And as within the little rose you find the richest dyes,
And in the little grain of gold much price and value lies,
As from a little balsam much odor doth arise,
So in a little woman there's a taste of paradise.

Como rubí pequeño tiene mucha bondad,
color, virtud y precio y noble claridad,
así dueña pequeña tiene mucha beldad,
hermosura, donaire, amor y lealtad.

Chica es la calandria y chico el ruiseñor,
pero más dulce canta que otra ave mayor;
la mujer, por ser chica, por eso no es peor;
con doñeo es más dulce que azúcar ni flor.

Son aves pequeñuelas papagayo y orior,
pero cualquier de ellas es dulce gritador,
adonada, hermosa, preciada cantador:
bien atal es la dueña pequeña con amor.

De la mujer pequeña no hay comparación,
terrenal paraíso es y gran consolación,
solaz y alegría, placer y bendición,
mejor es en la pueba que en la salutación.

Siempre quis mujer chica más que grande ni mayor,
no es desaguisado del gran mal ser huidor,
del mal tomar lo menos, dícelo el sabidor:
por ende de las mujeres la mejor es la menor.

Even as a little ruby its secret worth betrays,
Color and price and virtue, in the clearness of its rays,—
Just so a little woman much excellence displays,
Beauty and grace and love and fidelity always.

The skylark and the nightingale, though small and light of
    wing
Yet warble sweeter in the grove than all the birds that sing;
And so a little woman, though a very little thing,
Is sweeter far than sugar and flowers that bloom in spring.

The magpie and the golden thrush have many a thrilling note
Each as a gay musician doth strain his little throat,
A merry little songster in his green and yellow coat;
And such a little woman is, when Love doth make her dote.

There's naught can be compared to her, throughout the wide
    creation;
She is a paradise on earth,—our greatest consolation,—
So cheerful, gay and happy, so free from all vexation;
In fine, she's better in the proof than in anticipation.

If as her size increases are woman's charms decreased,
Then surely it is good to be from all the great released.
Now of two evils choose the less—said a wise man of the East,
By consequence, of woman-kind be sure to choose the least.

Marqués de Santillana (1398-1458)

Canción de amor

Si tú deseas a mí
yo no lo sé;
pero yo deseo a ti
en buena fe.

Ca no a ninguna más,
así lo ten;
ni es, ni será jamás
otra mi bien.
En tan buen hora te vi
y te hablé,
que del todo te me di
en buena fe.

Yo soy tuyo, no lo dudes
sin fallir;
y no pienses al, ni cudes
sin mentir.
Después que te conocí
me cautivé,
y seso y saber perdí
en buena fe.

A ti amo y amaré
toda sazón,
y siempre te serviré
con gran razón:
pues la mejor escogí
de cuantas sé,
y no finjo ni fingí
en buena fe.

Song of Love

Whether you love me,
I cannot declare;
But that I love you,
This I do swear.

No other woman
Could I hold so dear;
Not now, nor ever,
Another revere.
When I beheld you, Oh day
Most blest by love's tender prayer,
With my all I endowed you,
This I do swear.

I'm yours, don't doubt it,
So fear no deceit;
To think otherwise,
Would be false conceit.
Since the day I first met you,
My heart is caught in a snare,
And my wits are your captive,
This I do swear.

I love, will love you
Now and evermore;
Will serve you ever
By love's faithful law.
For I've chosen the finest
From amongst all the most fair,
And as truth is my witness,
This I do swear.

Juan de Mena (1411-1456)

Cantar de Macías

Amores me dieron corona de amores
porque mi nombre por más bocas ande.
Entonces no era mi mal menos grande
cuando me daban placer sus dolores.
Vencen el seso los dulces errores,
mas no duran siempre según luego placen;
pues me hicieron del mal que vos hacen,
sabed al amor desamar, amadores.
Fue un peligro tan apasionado;
sabed ser alegres; dejad de ser tristes.
Sabed deservir a quien tanto servistes,
a otro que amor da vuestro cuidado;
los cuales, si diesen por un igual grado
sus pocos placeres según su dolor,
no se quejara ningún amador,
ni desesperara ningún desamado,
de allí adelante vivir ya mejor,
mas desque pasado por él el temor,
vuelve a sus vicios como de primero.
Y bien como cuando algún malhechor,
al tiempo que hacen de otro justicia,
temor de la pena le pone codicia
así me volvieron a do desespero
deseos que quieren que muera amador.

Macias' Song

Love crowned me with his myrtle crown; my name
Will be pronounced by many, but, alas,
When his pangs caused me bliss, not slighter woe
The mournful suffering that consumed my frame!
His sweet snares conquer the lorn mind they tame,
But do not always then continue sweet;
And since they cause me ruin so complete,
Turn, lovers, turn, and disesteem his frame;
Dangers so passionate be glad to miss;
Learn to be gay; flee from sorrow's touch;
Learn to disserve him you have served so much,
Your devoirs pay to any shrine but his:
If the short joy that in his service is,
Were but proportioned to the long, long pain,
Neither would he that once has loved complain,
Nor he that ne'er has loved despair of bliss.
But even as some assassin or night-rover,
Seeing his fellow wound upon the wheel,
Awed by the agony resolves with zeal
His life to 'mend, and character recover;
But when the fearful spectacle is over,
Reacts his crimes with easy unconcern;
So my amours on my despair return,
That I should die, as I have lived, a lover!

Gil Vicente (1470?-1536?)

Dicen que me case yo

Dicen que me case yo:
no quiero marido, no.

Más quiero vivir segura
nesta sierra a mi soltura,
que no estar en ventura
si casaré bien o no.
Dicen que me case yo:
no quiero marido, no.

Madre, no seré casada
por no ver vida cansada,
o quizá mal empleada
la gracia que Dios me dio.
Dicen que me case yo:
no quiero marido, no.

No será ni es nacido
tal para ser mi marido;
y pues que tengo sabido
que la flor yo me la só,
dicen que me case yo:
no quiero marido, no.

Ode to Maidenhood

They say the marriage knot I should tie,
But I'll take no husband, no, not I.

More, I would rather live at my ease,
In these hills doing just as I please,
Than the hazards of fortune to sieze;
Such chance in wedlock I will defy:
They say the marriage knot I should tie,
But I'll take no husband, no, not I.

Mother, a wife I will never be,
A drudge's life I want not to see,
Nor the gifts with which God endowed me,
Perchance badly used as I comply:
They say the marriage knot I should tie,
But I'll take no husband, no, not I.

There does not, nor will ever exist
Such to catch me in some wedding tryst,
For as I well know and fain insist,
I, fully flowered, alone shall lie:
They say the marriage knot I should tie,
But I'll take no husband, no, not I.

Vanse mis amores

Vanse mis amores, madre,
luengas tierras van morar.
Yo no los puedo olvidar.
¿Quién me los hará tornar?
¿Quién me los hará tornar?

Yo soñaba, madre, un sueño
que me dio en el corazón:
que se iban los mis amores
a las islas de la mar.
Yo no los puedo olvidar.
¿Quién me los hará tornar?

Yo soñara, madre, un sueño
que me dio en el corazón:
que se iban los mis amores
a las tierras de Aragón.
Allá se van a morar.
Yo no los puedo olvidar.
¿Quién me los hará tornar?

My love has gone

Mother dear, my love has gone
To distant lands there to die.
I can't forget, hear my plea:
Who will bring him back to me?
Who will bring him back to me?

Mother dear, I had a dream,
It rent my heart to the core:
That my love would go away
To isles far across the sea.
I can't forget, hear my plea:
Who will bring him back to me?

Mother dear, I had a dream,
It rent my heart to the core:
That my love would go away
To Aragon's lands, I'm sure.
There his cruel death to see.
I can't forget, hear my plea:
Who will bring him back to me?

Fernando de Rojas (1475?-1541)

Lucero del día

Dulces árboles sombrosos,
humillaos cuando veáis
aquellos ojos graciosos
del que tanto desáis.

Estrellas que relumbráis
norte y lucero del día,
¿por qué no le despertáis,
si duerme mi alegría?

Canción de alborada

Papagayos, ruiseñores,
que cantáis al alborada,
llevad nueva a mis amores,
cómo espero aquí sentada.

La media noche es pasada,
y no viene.
Sabedme si hay otra amada
que lo detiene.

Venus Dawning

Gracious trees with your leafy shade,
Bow your heads when you see perchance
Those lovely eyes your bower invade,
And hold your jealousy in trance.

Stars whose shaft doth glitter and gleam,
Light that guides as Venus dawning,
Will you not rouse him from his dream,
If he slumbers fast this morning?

Song of Dawn

Chattering parrots, nightingales,
What songs you sing to greet the dawn!
Bring me news of my love's travails,
As I wait silent and forlorn.

The midnight hour has past 'er long
But still no sign of thee.
Tell me if another's blithe song
Keeps him away from me.

Cristóbal de Castillejo (1490?-1550)

Al Amor

Dame, Amor, besos sin cuento,
asido de mis cabellos,
y mil y ciento tras ellos,
y tras ellos mil y ciento,
y después
de muchos millares, tres;
y porque nadie los sienta,
desbaratemos la cuenta
y contemos al revés.

Aquel caballero

Aquel caballero, madre,
como a mí le quiero yo
y remedio no le dó.

El me quiere más que a sí,
yo le mato de cruel;
mas en serlo contra él
también lo soy contra mí.
De verle penar así
muy penada vivo yo,
y remedio no le dó.

To Love

Give me, Love, kisses without end,
Intertwined as hairs on my head,
A thousand and one kisses send;
Then yet a further thousand shed,
And after
Many thousands, another three.
Now, lest some prying eyes should see,
Let us in vain scratch out the score,
And recount backwards, as before.

That noble youth

Oh mother dear, that noble youth
I love such as my life, you know,
Yet to him no hope do I show.

He loves me above self, 'tis true,
Though with disdain I slay his heart,
But hurting him I reap my due,
As hurt to myself I impart.
To see him suffer such, forsooth,
My life in sorrow too does grow,
Yet to him no hope do I show.

Olvidar es lo mejor

En las dolencias de amor,
de pesar o de placer,
al que lo puede hacer,
olvidar es lo mejor.

Es amor una locura
de tristeza o de alegría,
que con memoria se cría
y con olvidar se cura;
el hurgarle es lo peor,
porque para guarecer
al que lo puede hacer,
olvidar es lo mejor.

'Tis better to forget

With love's most woeful debt,
Whether pain or pleasure,
When weighed by good measure,
'Tis better to forget.

Love is a madness, to be sure,
Whether it be sadness or joy,
And nurtured by memory's ploy,
Only forgetting can inure.
To scratch it with danger's beset,
For while clinging to life's treasure,
When weighed by good measure,
'Tis better to forget.

Garcilaso de la Vega (1503-1536)

Soneto

Escrito está en mi alma vuestro gesto

Escrito está en mi alma vuestro gesto,
y cuanto yo escribir de vos deseo;
vos sola lo escribisteis, yo lo leo
tan solo, que aún de vos me guardo en esto.

En esto estoy y estaré siempre puesto;
que aunque no cabe en mí cuanto en vos veo,
de tanto bien lo que no entiendo creo,
tomando ya la fe por presupuesto.

Yo no nací sino para quereros;
mi alma os ha cortado a su medida;
por hábito del alma misma os quiero.

Cuanto tengo confieso yo deberos;
por vos nací, por vos tengo la vida,
por vos he de morir, y por vos muero.

Sonnet

Thy face is written in my soul

Lady, thy face is written in my soul,
And whenso'er I wish to chant thy praise,
On that illumined manuscript I gaze,
Thou the sweet scribe art, I but read the scroll.
In this dear study all my days shall roll;
And though this book can ne'er the half receive
Of what in thee is charming, I believe
In that I see not, and thus see the whole
With faith's clear eye; I but received my breath
To love thee, my ill Genius shaped the rest;
'Tis now that soul's mechanic act to love thee,
I love thee, owe thee more than I confessed;
I gained life by thee, cruel though I prove thee;
In thee I live, through thee I bleed to death.

Egloga Primera

Nemoroso

¿Dó están ahora aquellos claros ojos
que llevaban tras sí como colgada
mi alma doquier que ellos se volvían?
¿Dó está la blanca mano delicada,
llena de vencimientos y despojos
que de mí mis sentimientos le ofrecían?
Los cabellos que vían
con gran desprecio el oro,
como a menor tesoro,
¿adónde están? ¿Adónde el blando pecho?
¿Dó la columna que el dorado techo
con presunción graciosa sostenía?
Aquesto todo ahora ya se encierra,
por desventura mía,
en la fría, desierta y dura tierra.

¿Quién me dijera, Elisa, vida mía,
cuando en aqueste valle al fresco viento
andábamos cogiendo tiernas flores,
que había de ver con largo apartamiento
venir el triste y solitario día
que diese amargo fin a mis amores?
El cielo en mis dolores
cargó la mano tanto,
que a sempiterno llanto
y a triste soledad me ha condenado;

Eclogue I

Nemoroso

Where are the eloquent mild eyes that drew
My heart where'er they wandered? where the hand,
White, delicate, and pure as melting dew,
Filled with the spoils that, proud of thy command,
My feelings paid in tribute? the bright hair
That paled the shining gold, that did contemn
The glorious opal as a meaner gem,
The bosom's ivory apples, where, ah where?
Where now the neck, to whiteness overwrought,
That like a column with genteelest scorn
Sustained the golden dome of virtuous thought?
Gone! ah, forever gone
To the chill, desolate, and dreary pall,
And mine the grief—the wormwood and the gall.

Who would have said, my love, when late through this
Romantic valley, we from bower to bower
Went gathering violets and primroses,
That I should see the melancholy hour
So soon arrive that was to end my bliss,
And of my love destroy both fruit and flower?
Heaven on my head has laid a heavy hand;
Sentencing, without hope, without appeal,
To loneliness and ever-during tears
The joyless remnant of my future years;

y lo que siento más es verme atado
a la pesada vida y enojosa,
solo, desamparado,
ciego, sin lumbre en cárcel tenebrosa.

. . . . .

Divina Elisa, pues ahora el cielo
con inmortales pies pisas y mides,
y su mudanza ves, estando queda,
¿por qué de mí te olvidas, y no pides
que se apresure el tiempo en que este velo
rompa del cuerpo, y verme libre pueda,
y en la tercera rueda
contigo mano a mano
busquemos otro llano,
busquemos otros montes y otros ríos,
otros valles floridos y sombríos,
donde descanse, y siempre pueda verte
ante los ojos míos,
sin miedo y sobresalto de perderte?

. . . . .

But that which most I feel,
Is to behold myself obliged to bear
This condemnation to a life of care;
Lone, blind, forsaken, under sorrow's spell,
A gloomy captive in a gloomy cell.

. . . . .

Divine Eliza, since the sapphire sky
Thou measurest now on angel-wings, the feet
Sandalled with immortality, oh why
Of me forgetful? Wherefore not entreat
To hurry on the time when I shall see
The veil of mortal being rent in twain,
And smile that I am free?
In the third circle of that happy land,
Shall we not seek together, hand in hand,
Another lovelier landscape, a new plain,
Other romantic streams and mountains blue,
Fresh flowery vales, and a new shady shore,
Where I may rest, and ever in my view
Keep thee, without the terror and surprise
Of being sundered more!

. . . . .

Santa Teresa de Jesús (1515-1582)

Vivo sin vivir en mí

Vivo sin vivir en mí,
y de tal manera espero,
que muero porque no muero.

Vivo ya fuera de mí,
después que muero de amor;
porque vivo en el Señor,
que me quiso para sí:
cuando el corazón le di
puso en él este letrero,
que muero porque no muero.

Esta divina prisión,
del amor con que yo vivo,
ha hecho a Dios mi cautivo,
y libre mi corazón;
y causa en mi tal pasión
ver a Dios mi prisionero,
que muero porque no muero.

¡Ay, qué larga es esta vida!
¡Qué duros estos destierros!
¡Esta cárcel, estos hierros
en que el alma está metida!
Sólo esperar la salida
me causa dolor tan fiero,
que muero porque no muero.

. . . . .

I die because I do not die

I live but not within myself,
And in this way awaiting lie:
I die because I do not die.

I live a life not truly mine,
Knowing I die of love's accord,
Because I live for Thee, my Lord;
And as Thou wanted me for Thine,
My heart to Thee I did consign,
Whence it released this aching sigh:
I die because I do not die.

This worldly prison cell divine,
Cell of love within which I live,
Has rendered God as my captive,
And frees my heart which did repine,
And does such passion in me enshrine.
Now God's my prisoner I cry:
I die because I do not die.

How wearisome this earthly life!
How hard to languish in exile!
This prison cell, these chains so vile,
In which this soul endures such strife!
Full yearning to leave my heart's rife
With pain so fierce that I reply:
I die because I do not die.

. . . . .

Si el amor que me tenéis

Si el amor que me tenéis,
Dios mío, es como el que os tengo,
decidme, ¿en qué me detengo?
O Vos, ¿en qué os detenéis?

—Alma, ¿qué quieres de mí?
Dios mío, no más que verte.
—¿Y qué temes más de ti?
Lo que más temo es perderte.

Un amor que ocupe os pido,
Dios mío, mi alma os tenga,
para hacer un dulce nido
adonde más la convenga.

Un alma en Dios escondida,
¿qué tiene que desear
sino amar y más amar
y en amor toda encendida
tornarte de nuevo a amar?

If the love Thou hast for me

If the love Thou hast for me, Lord,
Is equal to my love for Thee,
Tell me why should life detain me?
And Thou, why dost me life afford?

—Soul, what requesteth thou of me?
Dear Lord, only to see Thy face.
—And what dost thou most fear from thee?
What I most fear's to lose Thy grace.

Love all possessing is my quest,
Lord, take my heart and make it Thine,
Within Thy bosom build a nest,
In a spot that meets Thy design.

My soul in God hidden so deep,
What else is left for it to crave,
But to love Thee more as Thy slave,
And in so loving, so to sleep,
Starting afresh Thy love to save?

Gaspar Gil Polo (1517-1591)

No puedo no os querer

Si os pesa de ser querida,
yo no puedo no os querer,
pesar habréis de tener
mientras yo tuviere vida.

Sufrid que pueda quejarme,
pues que sufro un tal tormento,
o cumplid vuestro contento,
con acabar de matarme.
Que según sois descreída,
y os ofende mi querer,
pesar habréis de tener
mientras yo tuviere vida.

Si pudiendo conoceros,
pudiera dejar de amaros,
quisiera, por no enojaros,
poder dejar de quereros.
Mas pues vos seréis querida
mientras yo podré querer,
pesar habréis de tener
mientras yo tuviere vida.

I cannot cease to love

If it distress thee to be loved,
Why—as I cannot cease to love thee—
Learn thou to bear the thought unmoved,
Till death remove me, or remove thee.

O let me give feelings vent!
The melancholy thoughts that fill me;
Or send thy mandate; be content
To wound my inner heart, and kill me;
If love, whose smile would fain caress thee,
If love offend, yet why reprove?
I cannot, lady! but distress thee,
Because I cannot cease to love.

If I could check the passion glowing
Within my bosom,—if I could,
On other maids my love bestowing,
Give thy soul peace, sweet girl! I would.
But no! my heart cannot address thee
In aught but love!—then why reprove?
I cannot, lady! but distress thee,
Because I cannot cease to love.

Baltasar del Alcázar (1530-1606)

Soneto

La mujer celosa

Ningún hombre se llame desdichado
aunque le siga el hado ejecutivo,
supuesto que en Argel viva cautivo,
o al remo en las galeras condenado.
Ni el propio loco por furioso atado,
ni el que perdido llora estado altivo,
ni el que a deshonra trajo el tiempo esquivo,
o la necesidad a humilde estado.
Sufrid cualquiera pena es fácil cosa,
que ninguna atormentada tan de veras
que no la venza el sufrimiento un tanto.
Mas el que tiene la mujer celosa,
ése tiene desdicha, Argel, galeras,
locura, perdición, deshonra y llanto.

Sonnet

Woman's jealousy

Talk not to me of all the frowns of fate,
Or adverse fortune; nor offend my ears
With tales of slavery's suffering in Algiers,
Nor galley's chains, heavy, disconsolate.
Speak not to me of fetter'd maniacs' woes,
Nor proud one from his glory tumbled down:
Dimm'd honour,—friend-abandon'd,—broken crown:
These may be heavy sorrows; but who knows
To bend his head beneath the storms of life
With holy patience,—he the shock will bear,
And see the thundering clouds disperse away.
But give to mortal man a jealous wife,—
Then misery,—galleys,—fetters,—frowns,—dispair,—
loss,—shame,—dishonour,—folly:—What are they?

Soneto

Alma bella

Alma bella, que en este oscuro velo
cubriste un tiempo tu vigor luciente
y, en hondo y ciego olvido, gravemente
fuiste escondida sin alzar el vuelo.
Ya, despreciando este lugar, do el cielo
te encerró y apuró con fuerza ardiente,
y, roto el mortal nudo, vas presente
a eterna paz, dejando en guerra el suelo.
Vuelve tu luz a mí, y del centro tira
al ancho cerco de immortal belleza,
como vapor terrestre levantado
este espíritu opreso, que suspira
en vano por huir de esta estrecheza,
que impide estar contigo descansado.

Sonnet

Pure spirit

Pure Spirit! that within a form of clay
Once veiled the brightness of thy native sky;
In dreamless slumber sealed thy burning eye,
Nor heavenward sought to wing thy flight away!
He that chastised thee did at length unclose
Thy prison doors, and give thee sweet release,
Unloosed the mortal coil, eternal peace
Received thee to its stillness and repose.
Look down once more from thy celestial dwelling,
Help me to rise and be immortal there—
An earthly vapor melting into air;—
For my whole soul with secret ardor swelling,
From earth's dark mansion struggles to be free,
And longs to soar away and be at rest with thee.

San Juan de la Cruz (1542-1591)

Canción entre el Alma y el Esposo

Esposa

¿Adónde te escondiste,
Amado, y me dejaste con gemido?
Como el ciervo huiste,
habiéndome herido;
salí tras ti clamando, y eras ido.

Pastores, los que fuerdes
allá por las majadas al otero,
si por ventura vierdes
aquel que yo más quiero,
decidle que adolezco, peno y muero.

Buscando mis amores,
iré por esos montes y riberas;
ni cogeré las flores,
ni temeré las fieras,
y pasaré los fuertes y fronteras.

. . . . .

Song between The Soul and Her Bridegroom

The Bride

Whither hidest thou from me,
Beloved, and I left here grieving and wan?
Like flitting hart thou didst flee,
Leaving me wounded; anon
I ran after thee calling, but thou wert gone.

Shepherds, those of ye who've been
Watching over thy folds on yonder hill high,
If perchance ye might have seen
Him whom I most love go by;
Let him know that in anguish I pine and die.

Seeking my love I scour
The hills and dales, as I travel far and near;
But I shall pluck no flower,
Nor savage beast shall I fear;
Boldly I'll traverse all fortress and frontier.

. . . . .

Esposo

La blanca palomica
al arca con el ramo se ha tornado;
y ya la tortolica
al socio deseado
en las riberas verdes ha hallado.

En soledad vivía,
y en soledad ha puesto ya su nido,
y en soledad la guía
a solas su querido,
también en soledad de amor herido.

Esposa

Gocémonos, Amado,
y vámonos a ver en tu hermosura
al monte o al collado,
do mana el agua pura;
entremos más adentro en la espesura.

Y luego a las subidas
cavernas de la piedra nos iremos,
que están bien escondidas,
y allí nos entraremos,
y el mosto de granadas gustaremos.

. . . . .

The Bridegroom

Again the little white dove
To the ark with an olive branch has returned,
Already this turtle-dove
Her mate, for whom she so yearned,
On yonder green river bank has discerned.

Alone she has resided,
And in solitude she has built her nest,
And alone she is guided
By the one who loves her best,
Who in turn is wounded by love's lonely quest.

The Bride

Let us revel, Oh Dearest,
And may the mirror of thy loveliness show
The mountain and fell most blest,
Where the purest waters flow;
Let's go further into the thicket below.

Then soaring in altitude,
We shall take to the cavernous stony height,
Hidden in dense solitude,
Entering well out of sight,
In new pomegranate wine we shall delight.

· · · · ·

Miguel de Cervantes (1547-1616)

Amor

Amor, cuando yo pienso
en el mal que me das, terrible y fuerte,
voy corriendo a la muerte,
pensando así acabar mi mal inmenso;

Mas en llegando al paso
que es puerto en este mar de mi tormento,
tanta alegría siento,
que la vida se esfuerza y no le paso.

Así el vivir me mata,
que la muerte me torna a dar la vida.
¡Oh condición no oída,
la que conmigo muerte y vida trata!

Love

O, love, when, sick of heart-felt grief,
I sigh, and drag thy cruel chain,
To death I fly, the sure relief
Of those who groan in ling'ring pain.

But, coming to the fatal gates,
The port in this my sea of woe,
The joy I feel new life creates,
And bids my spirits brisker flow.

Thus dying every hour I live,
And living I resign my breath:
Strange power of love, that thus can give
A dying life and living death!

Marinero soy del amor

Marinero soy del amor,
y en su piélago profundo
navego sin esperanza
de llegar a puerto alguno.

Siguiendo voy a una estrella
que desde lejos descubro
más bella y resplandeciente
que cuantas vio Palinuro.

Yo no sé adónde me guía,
y así navego confuso,
el alma al mirarla atenta,
cuidadosa y con descuido.

Recatos impertinentes,
honestidad contra el uso,
son nubes que me la encubren
cuando más verla procuro.

¡Oh clara y luciente estrella,
en cuya lumbre me apuro!
al punto que te me encubras,
será de mi muerte el punto.

Love's hapless mariner

Toss'd in a sea of doubts and fears,
Love's hapless mariner, I sail
Where no inviting port appears,
To screen me from the stormy gale.

At distance view'd, a cheering star
Conducts me through the swelling tide;
A brighter luminary far
Than Palinurus e'er descried.

My soul, attracted by its blaze,
Still follows where it points the way,
And, while attentively I gaze,
Considers not how far I stray.

But female pride, reserved and shy,
Like clouds that deepen on the day,
Oft shrouds it from my longing eye,
When most I need the guiding ray.

O, lovely star, so pure and bright!
Whose splendour feeds my vital fire,
The moment thou deny'st thy light,
Thy lost adorer will expire.

¿Quién menoscaba mis bienes?

¿Quién menoscaba mis bienes?
　　　Desdenes.
¿Y quién aumenta mis duelos?
　　　Los celos.
¿Y quién prueba mi paciencia?
　　　Ausencia.
De ese modo en mi dolencia
ningún remedio se alcanza,
pues me matan la esperanza,
desdenes, celos y ausencia.

¿Quién me causa este dolor?
　　　Amor.
¿Y quién mi gloria repugna?
　　　Fortuna.
¿Y quién consiente mi duelo?
　　　El cielo.
De este modo yo recelo
morir deste mal extraño,
pues se aunan en mi daño
amor, fortuna y el cielo.

¿Quién mejorará mi suerte?
　　　La muerte.
Y el bien de amor, ¿quién le alcanza?
　　　Mudanza.
Y sus males, ¿quién los cura?
　　　Locura.
De este modo no es cordura
querer curar la pasión,
cuando los remedios son:
muerte, mudanza y locura.

What causes all my grief and pain?

What causes all my grief and pain?
        Cruel disdain.
What aggravates my misery?
        Accursed jealousy.
How has my soul its patience lost?
        By tedious absence cross'd.
Alas! no balsam can be found
To heal the grief of such a wound.
When absence, jealousy and scorn,
Have left me hopeless and forlorn.

What in my breast this grief could move?
        Neglected love.
What doth my fond desires withstand?
        Fate's cruel hand.
What confirms my misery?
        Heaven's fix'd decree.
Ah me! my boding fears portend,
This strange disease my life will end:
For die I must, when three such foes,
Heav'n, fate, and love, my bliss oppose.

My peace of mind what can restore?
        Death's welcome hour.
What gains love's joys most readily?
        Fickle inconstancy.
Its pains what medicine can assuage?
        Wild phrenzy's rage.
'Tis therefore little wisdom, sure,
For such a grief to seek a cure,
That knows no better remedy
Than phrenzy, death, inconstancy.

Vicente Espinel (1550-1624)

Siempre alcanza lo que quiere

Siempre alcanza lo que quiere
con damas el atrevido,
y el que no es entrometido
de necio, y cobarde muere.

La honestidad en las damas
es un velo que les fuerza,
cuando amor tiene más fuerza,
a no descubrir sus llamas.
Por eso el que las sirviere,
cánsese por atrevido,
que el que no es entrometido
de necio, y cobarde muere.

Mil ocasiones hallamos
con las damas que queremos
y cuando más las tenemos,
de cortos no las gozamos,
pues mire el que amor tuviere,
que en el bando de Cupido
el que no es entrometido
de necio, y cobarde muere.

Faint heart never won fair lady

He who is both brave and bold
Wins the lady that he would;
But the courageless and cold
Never did, and never could.

Modesty, in woman's game,
Is a wide and shielding veil:
They are tutor'd to conceal
Passion's fiercely burning flame.
He who serves them brave and bold,
He alone is understood;
But the courageless and cold
Ne'er could win, and never should.

If you love a lady bright,
Seek—and you shall find a way;
All that love would say—to say—
If you watch the occasion right,
Cupid's ranks are brave and bold,
Every soldier firm and good;
But the courageless and cold
Ne'er have conquered—never could.

Anonymous (from *Silva de Romances* 17th century)

Mientras duerme la niña

Mientras duerme la niña,
flores y rosas,
azucenas y lirios
le hacen sombra.

En el prado verde
la niña reposa
donde Manzanares
sus arroyos brota.

No se mueve el viento,
ramas ni hojas,
que azucenas y lirios
le hacen sombra.

El sol la obedece
y su paso acorta,
que son rayos bellos
sus ojos y boca.

Las aves no cantan
viendo tal gloria,
que azucenas y lirios
le hacen sombra.

Amaryllis

She sleeps;—Amaryllis
Midst flowerets is laid;
And roses and lilies
Make the sweet shade.

The maiden is sleeping,
Where through the green hills,
Manzanares is creeping
Along with his rills.

Wake not Amaryllis,
Ye winds in the glade!
Where roses and lilies
Make the sweet shade.

The sun, while upsoaring,
Yet tarries awhile,
The bright rays adoring
Which stream from her smile.

The wood-music still is
To rouse her afraid,
Where roses and lilies
Make the sweet shade.

Luis de Góngora (1561-1627)

Soneto

Si amor...

Si amor entre las plumas de su nido
prendió mi libertad, ¿qué hará ahora,
que en tus ojos, dulcísima señora,
armado vuela, ya que no vestido?

Entre las violetas fui herido
del áspid que hoy entre los lilios mora;
igual fuerza tenías siendo aurora,
que ya como sol tienes bien nacido.

Saludaré tu luz con voz doliente,
cual tierno ruiseñor en prisión dura
despide quejas, pero dulcemente.

Diré cómo de rayos vi tu frente
coronada, y que hace tu hermosura
cantar las aves, y llorar la gente.

Sonnet

If love...

If Love, within the feathers of his nest,
Imprisoned my heart, what will he do now,
When in thy eyes, O Lady of sweet brow,
He flies in armour clad, though yet undressed?

I was stung, amid the violets pressed,
By the asp that lives midst the lilies' bough;
As fragrant Dawn equal power hadst thou
As now, when Sun, thou dost shimmer full crest.

I'll greet the light in grave voice rent with pain,
As the kind nightingale in prison bound
Gives voice to grievances with sweet refrain.

I'll tell how with rays I saw thy brow gain
A crown, and that thy loveliness renowned
Doth cause birds to sing and men tears attain.

Lope de Vega (1562-1635)

Si os partiéredes

Si os partiéredes al alba
quedito, pasito, amor,
no espantéis al ruiseñor.

Si os levantáis de mañana
de los brazos que os desean,
porque en los brazos no os vean
de alguna envidia liviana,
pisad con planta de lana,
quedito, pasito, amor,
no espantéis al ruiseñor.

Canción

(de *Fuenteovejuna*)

Vivan muchos años juntos
los novios, ruego a los cielos,
y por envidia ni celos
ni riñan ni anden en puntos.
Lleven a entrambos difuntos,
de puro vivir cansados.
¡Vivan muchos años!

If thou leavest

If thou leavest at dawn's first hail
Oh so quietly, slowly, love,
Do not startle the nightingale.

If thou wakest at break of day,
From these arms that desire thee e'en,
That thou, embraced, shouldst not be seen
In some covetous tryst alay.
Steal on fleecy tiptoe, sail
Oh so quietly, slowly, love,
Do not startle the nightingale.

Song

(from *Fuenteovejuna*)

A long life may they share as one,
The young lovers, this is my plea;
Let not envy or jealousy
Make them bicker or treat with scorn.
May they many relatives mourn,
Living so long in unison,
A long life may they share as one!

¿Quién mata con más rigor?

¿Quién mata con más rigor?
      Amor.
¿Quién causa tantos desvelos?
      Celos.
¿Quién es el mal de mi bien?
      Desdén.
¿Qué más que todos también
una esperanza perdida,
pues que me quiten la vida
amor, celos y desdén?

¿Qué fin tendrá mi osadía?
      Porfía.
Y ¿qué remedio mi daño?
      Engaño.
¿Quién es contrario a mi amor?
      Temor.
Luego es forzoso el rigor,
y locura el porfiar,
pues mal se pueden juntar
porfía, engaño y temor.

¿Qué es lo que el amor me ha dado?
      Cuidado.
Y ¿qué es lo que yo le pido?
      Olvido.
¿Qué tengo del bien que veo?
      Deseo.
Si en tal locura me empleo,

Who kills wearing cruelty's glove?

Who kills wearing cruelty's glove?
          Love.
On what fare does restlessness feed?
          Jealousy's seed.
With what ill is my dearest torn?
          Scorn.
What, moreo'er, do such forces spawn,
But a life without hope and joy,
For three things my being destroy,
By name: love, jealousy and scorn.

What result my bold existence?
          Persistence.
What end will my suffering meet?
          Deceit.
Who fights against my love so dear?
          Fear.
Perforce does cruelty appear,
And 'tis but madness to insist,
For the joining one should resist
Of: persistence, deceit and fear.

What emblem does love bid me wear?
          Care.
And what is it I most request?
          Oblivion's nest.
What does the good I see inspire?
          Desire.
Persisting in such madness dire

que soy mi propio enemigo,
presto acabarán conmigo,
cuidado, olvido y deseo.

Nunca mi pena fue dicha.
      Desdicha.
¿Qué aguarda mi pretensión?
      Ocasión.
¿Quién hace a amor resistencia?
      Ausencia.
Pues ¿dónde hallaré paciencia,
aunque a la muerte le pida,
si me han de acabar la vida
desdicha, ocasión y ausencia?

Linda casada

(de *Peribáñez*)

Cogiome a tu puerta el toro,
linda casada;
no dijiste: Dios te valga.
El novillo de tu boda
a tu puerta me cogió;
de la vuelta que me dio
se rio la villa toda;
y tú, grave y burladora,
linda casada,
no dijiste: Dios te valga.

That my enemy lies within,
Soon these horsemen will do me in:
Care, oblivion and desire.

My woe never brought happiness.
                    Unhappiness.
On what does my hope want to glance?
                    Chance.
What counters and thwarts love's essence?
                    Absence.
For where shall I find the patience,
Though of death I ask it in strife,
If these things end taking my life:
Unhappiness, chance and absence.

Comely wedded lass

(from *Peribáñez*)

When the bull gored me at your door,
Comely wedded lass,
Not e'en 'God help you' did you say.
When the steer of your wedding day
Caught me on your doorstep astray,
As he beat and pushed me around,
The village in laughter was drowned,
And you, so grave, mockingly frowned,
Comely wedded lass,
Not e'en 'God help you' did you say.

Amor que pierde el respeto

(de *El Mejor Alcalde, El Rey*)

Elvira:

> No, señor;
> que amor que pierde al honor
> el respeto, es vil deseo,
> y siendo apetito feo,
> no puede llamarse amor.
>   Amor se funda en querer
> lo que quiere quien desea;
> que amor que casto no sea,
> ni es amor ni puede ser.

Que yo por amor...

(de: *La Moza de Cántaro*)

Don Juan:

> Que yo por amor me case,
> que yo por amor me pierda,
> no es justo que a nadie admire,
> pues cuantos viven confiesan
> que es amor una pasión
> incapaz de resistencia.

Love that loses respect

(from *El Mejor Alcalde, El Rey*)

Elvira:

No, Sir;
Love that loses respect above
All for honour, is vile desire,
Being foul appetite so dire
It can never call itself love.
　Love is founded on holding dear
What lies in your loved one's desire;
Love impure can never acquire
The name love, and will ne'er adhere.

That I for love

(from *La Moza de Cántaro*)

Don Juan:

That I for love should marry this day,
That I for love should lose my senses,
'Tis unjust that you show this surprise:
All admit there are no defences,
Because love to such passion gives rise,
That it every resistance defies.

Francisco de Quevedo (1580-1645)

Soneto

Definiendo al Amor

Es yelo abrasador, es fuego helado,
es herida que duele y no se siente,
es un soñado bien, un mal presente,
es un breve descanso muy cansado.

Es un descuido que nos da cuidado,
un cobarde, con nombre de valiente,
un andar solitario entre la gente,
un amar solamente ser amado.

Es una libertad encarcelada,
que dura hasta el postrero parasismo;
enfermedad que crece si es curada.

Este es el niño Amor, éste es su abismo.
¡Mirad cuál amistad tendrá con nada
el que en todo es contrario de sí mismo!

Sonnet

Defining Love

It is scorching ice, it is freezing fire,
It is a painful wound that doth not ache,
A sweet dream, but bitterness when awake,
It is a brief repose that doth so tire.

A careless moment that doth care acquire,
It is a coward who brave name doth take,
A lonely walk among the crowd a quake,
A loving just to be loved, nought higher.

It is freedom to a prison cell lured,
That endures unto everlasting life,
An illness that worsens if it's cured.

This is young Cupid, his abyss is rife.
To all kinds of friendship he is inured,
He whom paradox has riven with strife.

Tirso de Molina (1584-1648)

Arminta, escucha

(de *El Burlador de Sevilla*)

Don Juan:

Arminta, escucha y sabrás,
si quieres que te la diga,
la verdad, si las mujeres
sois de verdades amigas.
Yo soy noble caballero,
cabeza de la familia
de los Tenorios antiguos,
ganadores de Sevilla.
Mi padre, después del Rey,
se reverencia y se estima
en la Corte, y de sus labios
penden las muertes y vidas.
Torciendo el camino acaso,
llegué a verte, que amor guía
tal vez las cosas de suerte
que él mismo de ellas se admira.
Vite, adoréte, abraséme,
tanto que tu amor me obliga
a que contigo me case.
Mira qué acción tan precisa.
Y aunque lo murmure el reino,
y aunque el Rey lo contradiga,
y aunque mi padre, enojado,
con amenazas lo impida,
tu esposo tengo de ser...

Oh Arminta, listen

(from *The Love-Rogue of Seville*)

Don Juan:

> Oh Arminta, listen to me,
> For I swear to tell thee no lie,
> If women verity honour,
> And the truth thou wouldst not deny.
> A gentleman of noble birth,
> Head of the family am I,
> Tenorios, landed gentry
> From Seville, of lineage high.
> After the King, to my father
> All respect and esteem comply
> At Court, and on his word doth hang
> Whether one is to live or die.
> Veering off my route, I happened
> To see thee, as Love brought me nigh,
> For he guides those things of fortune
> Which he doth deign to dignify.
> I saw thee, adored thee, I burned,
> Such that this love I feel doth ply
> Me humbly to pledge thee my troth.
> Such action must deceit belie.
> And though the realm may condemn it,
> And the King forbid it, Oh fie,
> And though my father, in anger,
> With threats his permission deny,
> Your husband I will surely be...

Al contemplar a Rosaura

(de *La Vida es Sueño*)

Segismundo:

Tu voz pudo enternecerme,
tu presencia suspenderme
y tu respeto turbarme.
¿Quién eres? que aunque yo aquí
tan poco del mundo sé,
que cuna y sepulcro fue
esta torre para mí;
y aunque desde que nací
(si esto es nacer) sólo advierto
este rústico desierto
donde miserable vivo,
siendo un esqueleto vivo,
siendo un animado muerto;
y aunque nunca vi ni hablé
sino a un hombre solamente
que quien mis desdichas siente,
por quien las noticias sé
de cielo y tierra; y aunque
aquí, por más que te asombres
y monstruo humano me nombres,
entre asombros y quimeras,
soy un hombre de las fieras
y una fiera de los hombres;

On seeing Rosaura

(from *Life is a Dream*)

Segismundo:
> Oh, how thy voice doth soothe me,
> And thy presence dazzle me,
> How thy respect pierces me!
> Who art thou? for I know nought
> Of the world outside this cell,
> A cradle and tomb unsought,
> This tower in which I dwell;
> And though since I am alive,
> (If this living be) I know
> Just this crude desert, Ah woe!
> In misery I survive
> Like some walking skeleton,
> Like some breathing corpse consigned;
> To speak and see I'm confined
> 'Er but to one man alone,
> Who all my sorrows hath known,
> And through whom I have all word
> Of heaven and earth; although
> Thou dost astonishment show,
> I'm a fiend of humans wrought,
> If to thee it seem absurd,
> I'm a man in a beast's den,
> And a wild beast among men;

y aunque en desdichas tan graves
la política he estudiado,
de los brutos enseñado,
advertido de las aves,
y de los astros suaves
los círculos he medido,
tú, sólo tú, has suspendido
la pasión a mis enojos,
la suspensión a mis ojos,
la admiración a mi oído.
Con cada vez que te veo
nueva admiración me das,
y cuando te miro más,
aún más mirarte deseo.
Ojos hidrópicos creo
que mis ojos deben ser:
pues, cuando es muerte el beber,
beben más, y desta suerte,
viendo que el ver me da muerte,
estoy muriendo por ver.
Pero véate yo y muera;
que no sé, rendido ya,
si el verte muerte me da,
el no verte qué me diera.
Fuera más que muerte fiera,
ira, rabia y dolor fuerte;
fuera muerte: desta suerte
su rigor he ponderado,
pues dar vida a un desdichado
es dar a un dichoso muerte.

Though with gravest sorrows fraught,
Life's vital lore I have learned,
By the brutes adeptly taught,
From the birds guidance discerned,
And of the stars' fine resort,
I've measured their heav'nly spheres;
Yet thee alone could arrest
The suffering in my breast,
The wonderment of my ears,
The amazement in my eyes.
Each time thy vision appears,
Fresh amazement in thy guise
Fills me, that the more I see,
More I want to gaze at thee.
I think a dropsy severe
Must have afflicted my eyes:
For, when drinking death implies,
They drink more, and show no fear,
As seeing thee brings death near,
I'm dying to see, 'tis clear.
Yet let me see thee and die;
I yield, for I do not know,
If seeing thee brings death nigh,
What not seeing thee'd bestow.
A fate worse than death most drear,
Anger, rage and pain severe;
Death it were: and delivered
Its rigours I've considered,
Since to give a wretch life's breath
Is to give the happy death.

Amor, amor

(de *El Mágico Prodigioso*)

Voz: ¿Cuál es la gloria mayor
de esta vida?

Todos: Amor, amor.

Voz: No hay sujeto en quien no imprima
el fuego de amor su llama,
pues vive más donde ama
el hombre, que donde anima.
Amor solamente estima
cuanto tener vida sabe,
el tronco, la flor y el ave:
luego en la gloria mayor
de esta vida.

Todos: Amor, amor.

Justina: Pesada imaginación,
al parecer lisonjera,
¿cuándo te he dado ocasión
para que desta manera
aflijas mi corazón?
¿Cuál es la causa, en rigor,
deste fuego, deste ardor,
que en mí por instantes crece?
¿Qué dolor el que padece
mi sentido?

Todos: Amor, amor.

Love, love

(from *El Mágico Prodigioso*)

A Voice Within:
What is the glory far above
All else in human life?

All: Love! love!

The First Voice:
There is no form in which the fire
Of love its traces has impressed not.
Man lives far more in love's desire
Than by life's breath, soon possessed not.
If all that lives must love or lie,
All shapes on earth, or sea, or sky,
With one consent, to Heaven cry
That the glory far above
All else in life is—

All: Love! O, love!

Justina: Thou melancholy thought, which art
So fluttering and so sweet, to thee
When did I give the liberty
Thus to afflict my heart?
What is the cause of this new power
Which doth my fevered being move,
Momently raging more and more?
What subtle pain is kindled now,
Which from my heart doth overflow
Into my senses?

All: Love! O, love!

Gustavo Adolfo Bécquer (1836-1870)

Rima XI

Yo soy ardiente

Yo soy ardiente, yo soy morena,
yo soy el símbolo de la pasión,
de ansia de goces mi alma está llena;
¿a mí me buscas?
     —No es a ti; no.

Mi frente es pálida, mis trenzas de oro,
puedo brindarte dichas sin fin,
yo de ternuras guardo un tesoro;
¿a mí me llamas?
     —No; no es a ti.

Yo soy un sueño, un imposible,
vano fantasma de niebla y luz,
soy incorpórea, soy intangible;
no puedo amarte.
     —¡Oh ven; ven tú!

Rima XVII

Hoy la tierra y los cielos

Hoy la tierra y los cielos me sonríen,
hoy llega al fondo de mi alma el sol,
hoy la he visto... la he visto y me ha mirado...
¡hoy creo en Dios!

Rhyme XI

I am dusky, I am a flame

I am dusky, I am a flame
I am the symbol of passion,
Brimful pleasure my soul doth claim;
Thou seekest me?
                        —No, not thee.

My brow is pale, my tresses gold,
I offer thee abiding joys,
Of tenderness, I treasures enfold;
Thou callest me?
                        —No, not thee.

I am a dream, inpalpable,
A vague phantom of mist and light,
Disembodied, I'm intangible;
I cannot love thee.
                        —O, come! come to me!

Rhyme XVII

Today heaven and earth

Today heaven and earth smile on me,
Today, with the sun's rays my soul is shot,
Today I saw her... I saw her and she gave me a glance...
Today I believe in God!

Rima XXI

¿Qué es poesía?

¿Qué es poesía?, dices mientras clavas
en mi pupila tu pupila azul.
¡Qué es poesía! ¿Y tú me lo preguntas?
Poesía... eres tú.

Rima XXII

¿Cómo vive esa rosa?

¿Cómo vive esa rosa que has prendido
junto a tu corazón?
Nunca hasta ahora contemplé en el mundo
junto al volcán la flor.

Rima XXIII

Por una mirada

Por una mirada, un mundo;
por una sonrisa, un cielo;
por un beso... yo no sé
que te diera por un beso.

Rhyme XXI

What is poetry?

What is poetry?, you say
As you fix my eyes with yours of blue.
What is poetry!... You ask me that?
Poetry... It is you!

Rhyme XXII

How liveth next to thy heart?

How liveth next to thy heart
That rose so tightly clasped?
A flower next to a volcano till now
I never saw in this world so vast.

Rhyme XXIII

For a glance

For a glance: the world;
For a smile: the heavens;
For a kiss... I don't know
What I'd give for a kiss!

Rima XXX

Asomaba a sus ojos

Asomaba a sus ojos una lágrima
y a mi labio una frase de perdón;
habló el orgullo y se enjugó su llanto,
y la frase en mis labios expiró.

Yo voy por un camino; ella, por otro;
pero al pensar en nuestro mutuo amor,
yo digo aún: ¿por qué callé aquel día?
Y ella dirá: ¿por qué no lloré yo?

Rima XXXVIII

Los suspiros son aire

Los suspiros son aire y van al aire.
Las lágrimas son agua y van al mar.
Dime, mujer: cuando el amor se olvida,
¿sabes tú adónde va?

Rhyme XXX

A tear swelled up

Within her eye a tear swelled up,
And a word of forgiveness on my lips hung;
Pride then spoke and stifled her sob,
And the word expired on my tongue.

I take one path, she another;
But, thinking on our love once deep,
I still ask: why did I not speak that day?
And she asks: why did I not weep?

Rhyme XXXVIII

Sighs are air

Sighs are air and go to the air.
Tears are water and to the sea flow.
Tell me, woman: knowest thou,
When love's forgot, where it doth go?

Rima LXXVII

Dices que tienes corazón

Dices que tienes corazón, y sólo
lo dices porque sientes sus latidos;
eso no es corazón... es una máquina
que al compás que se mueve hace ruido.

Rima LXXXI

Amor eterno

Podrá nublarse el sol eternamente;
podrá secarse en un instante el mar;
podrá romperse el eje de la tierra
como un débil cristal.

¡Todo sucederá! Podrá la muerte
cubrirme con un fúnebre crespón;
pero jamás en mí podrá apagarse
la llama de tu amor.

Rhyme LXXVII

You say you have a heart

You say you have a heart, and you say
It only because you feel it beat;
That is not a heart... but a machine
Which marks time to its noise of pulse neat.

Rhyme LXXXI

Eternal love

The sun could cast an eternal shadow,
And the sea could run dry in but a chime;
The earth's axis could break
Like crystal fine.

Anything could happen! Death enswathing
Could cover me with its mournful attire;
But in me your love's flame
Could ne'er expire.

Rosalía de Castro (1837-1885)

Te amo... ¿Por qué me odias?

Te amo... ¿Por qué me odias?
—Te odio... ¿Por qué me amas?
Secreto es éste el más triste
y misterioso del alma.

Mas ello es verdad... ¡Verdad
dura y atormentadora!
—Me odias porque te amo;
te amo, porque me odias.

I love you... Why do you hate me?

I love you... Why do you hate me?
—I hate you... Why do you love me?
A sad and most mysterious
Secret of the heart is this.

Yet it is true... An arduous
And excruciating truth!
—You hate me, because I love you;
I love you, because you hate me.

Antonio Machado (1875-1939)

Amada, el aura dice...

Amada, el aura dice
tu pura veste blanca...
No te verán mis ojos;
¡mi corazón te aguarda!

El viento me ha traído
tu nombre en la mañana;
el eco de tus pasos
repite la montaña...
No te verán mis ojos;
¡mi corazón te aguarda!

En las sombrías torres
repican las campanas...
No te verán mis ojos;
¡mi corazón te aguarda!

Los golpes del martillo
dicen la negra caja;
y el sitio de la fosa,
los golpes de la azada...
No te verán mis ojos;
¡mi corazón te aguarda!

My love, the breeze brings me word

My love, the breeze brings me word
Of thy gown of purest white...
My eyes will ne'er more see thee;
But my heart awaits thy light!

The balmy wind has borne me
Thy name this morning bright;
The echo of thy footsteps
Resounds on the mountain's height...
My eyes will ne'er more see thee;
But my heart awaits thy light!

In the shadowy towers,
The bells toll their doleful rite...
My eyes will ne'er more see thee;
But my heart awaits thy light!

The hammer blows speak loudly
Of the coffin dark as night;
And the graveside resonates
With the sound of the spade's might...
My eyes will ne'er more see thee;
But my heart awaits thy light!

En la calle sombría

La calle en sombra. Ocultan los altos caserones
el sol que muere; hay ecos de luz en los balcones.

¿No ves, en el encanto del mirador florido,
el óvalo rosado de un rostro conocido?

La imagen, tras el vidrio de equívoco reflejo,
surge o se apaga como daguerrotipo viejo.

Suena en la calle sólo el ruido de tu paso;
se extinguen lentamente los ecos del ocaso.

¡Oh angustia! Pesa y duele el corazón... ¿Es ella?
No puede ser... Camina... En el azul, la estrella.

Señor, ya me arrancaste

Señor, ya me arrancaste lo que yo más quería.
Oye otra vez, Dios mío, mi corazón clamar.
Tu voluntad se hizo, Señor, contra la mía,
Señor, ya estamos solos mi corazón y el mar.

The street in shade

The street in shade. The rooftops high of old houses now veil
The dying sun; echoes of light over balconies sail.

Can't you see, midst that charming window with flowers inset,
The rose-coloured oval of a visage remembered yet?

The reflection, in a pane of equivocal image,
Surges and fades like some daguerreotype of old vintage.

In the stillness of the street only your footsteps are heard;
The remaining echoes of twilight slowly become blurred.

Oh anguish! My heavy heart aches... Can it perchance be she?
It cannot be... Walk on... In the blue above, a star I see.

Lord, Thou didst wrench

Lord, Thou didst wrench from me what I most cherished.
Dear God, hear once more my heart's pitiful groan.
Thy will was done, Lord, against what I most wished,
My heart and the sea, Lord, are now left alone.

Spanish Quotations and Proverbs

Obras son amores, que no buenas razones.

Proverb

Todo en amor es triste;
mas triste y todo,
es lo mejor que existe.

Proverb

¿Por qué amas la dueña que no te precia nada?
Corazón, por tu culpa, vivirás vida penada.

Arcipreste de Hita

Ama y serás amado y podrás
hacer lo que no harás desamado.

Marqués de Santillana

¡Cuántos vi ser aumentados por amor,
y muchos más por temor abajados!

Marqués de Santillana

La niña que amores ha,
sola, ¿cómo dormirá?

Marqués de Santillana

Love is works, not words.

In love all is sadness;
but sadness and all,
it's still the best thing in life.

Why lovest thou the lady who feels nought for thee?
Dear heart, through thy own fault, a miserable life thou shalt
live.

Love and you will be loved, and you will be able
to do all that you could not do unloved.

How many people I've seen elevated by love,
and how many more diminished by fear!

A girl in love,
how can she sleep alone?

La mujer sin hombre, es como el fuego sin leña.

Proverb

El hombre es fuego, la mujer estopa;
llega el diablo y sopla.

Proverb

Que si yo no vos amara
y tanto bien no quisiera,
ni vuestro mal me penara,
ni vuestro bien me pluguiera.

Gómez Manrique

Es amor fuerza, tan fuerte,
que fuerza toda razón.

Jorge Manrique

Quiero dormir y no puedo
qu'el amor me quita el sueño.

from Romancero

Entra mayo con sus flores,
sale abril con sus amores
y los dulces amadores
comienzan a bien servir.

from Romancero

Woman without man is like fire without wood.

Man is fire, woman dry straw,
then the devil comes along and blows.

If I did not so love thee
and thy good keenly desire,
thy ill-fate would not grieve me,
nor thy good fortune please me.

Love is a power so powerful
that it overpowers all reason.

O how I wish I could sleep,
but in me love doth wakefulness steep.

May comes in with her flowers,
April leaves with her lovers,
and the charming young sweethearts
begin to play their parts.

En guerra, caza y amores,
por un placer mil dolores.

Proverb

Juramentos de amor y humo de chimenea,
el viento se los lleva.

Proverb

El alma, por lo que sufre;
la vida, por lo que padece; el corazón, por lo
que pasa; el sentido, por lo que siente.

Diego de San Pedro

Amor que no pena
no pida placer,
pues ya le condena
su poco querer.

Juan del Encina

Mi querer muy verdadero me forzó
a ser vuestro como só.

Juan del Encina

Si le manda matar, madre,
juntos nos han de enterrar.

from Romancero

In war, hunting and love,
a little pleasure gives a lot of pain.

Vows of love and smoke from the fireplace,
the wind blows them both away.

The soul is measured by how much it suffers;
life by how much it endures; the heart by how much
it grieves; and the senses by how much they feel.

A love without sorrow
pleasure should not claim,
for it is condemned
by its feeble flame.

My love most true
has made me yours.

Mother, if you order him to be killed,
they will have to bury us together.

Más vale pan con amor,
que gallina con dolor.

Proverb

Quien quiere a Beltrán,
quiere a su can.

Proverb

Agora que sé de amor,
¿me metéis monja?
¡Ay Dios, qué grave cosa!

from Cancionero

No quiero ser monja, no,
que niña namoradica só.

from Cancionero

Las mis penas, madre,
de amores son.

from Cancionero

Sepan cuantos son nacidos
aquesta sentencia mía:
que contra la muerte y amor
nadie no tiene valía.

Gil Vicente

It's better to eat dry bread in love,
than a feast in sorrow.

Love me, love my dog.

Now that I know of love,
you take me to the convent?
Dear God, what a sad event!

I don't want to be a nun, no,
for a girl in love am I.

All my sorrows, mother,
are of love's making.

Let all mortals know
of this my refrain:
that against death and love
all might is in vain.

Juran los enamorados
que todos tienen los ojos vendados.

Proverb

Quien bien quiere, tarde olvida.

Proverb

Juras del que ama mujer, no se han de creer.

Proverb

Remedio no espero
de mi pena grave;
perdióse la llave
¿do está lo que quiero?

Cristóbal de Castillejo

[Amor] Es un fuego escondido, una agradable llaga, un
sabroso veneno, una dulce amargura, una delectable dolencia,
un alegre tormento,
una dulce y fiera herida, una blanda muerte.

Fernando de Rojas

Si tu corazón siente lo que ahora el mío,
maravillada estoy cómo la ausencia te consiente vivir.

Fernando de Rojas

Lovers swear that everyone else is blind.

One who truly loves, finds it difficult to forget.

Vows of love, woman, should not be believed.

A solution I don't expect
to my grief so severe,
the key has now been lost,
where is the one I love most dear?

[Love] is a hidden fire, a pleasant sore, a delicious poison, a
sweet bitterness, a delectable pain, an agreeable torment, a
sweet and throbbing wound, a gentle death.

If your heart feels what mine now feels,
I am amazed how this absence permits you to live.

Quien bien te quiere, te hará llorar.

Proverb

Más fuerte era Sansón y le venció el amor.

Proverb

Por cierto, los gloriosos santos que se deleitan
en la visión divina, no gozan más
que yo ahora en el acatamiento tuyo.

Fernando de Rojas

¿Qué quieres que cante, amor mío?
¡Cómo cantaré, que tu deseo era el
que regía mi son y hacía sonar mi canto!

Fernando de Rojas

No me tienes que dar, porque te quiera;
que aunque cuanto espero no esperara,
lo mismo que te quiero te quisiera.

Santa Teresa de Jesús

Vuestra soy, para vos nací.

Santa Teresa de Jesús

The one who truly loves you will cause you pain.

Samson was stronger than you, and love defeated him.

I'm sure that the glorious saints who rejoice
in the divine countenance, know no more joy
than I now, worshipping you.

What would you like me to sing, my love?
How shall I sing, for your desire always
ruled my tone and made my singing tuneful!

I need no reward for this love I bear Thee,
for, though all my hopes in the end were in vain,
this love I have for Thee now would still remain.

I am Thine, for Thee I was born.

Corazón llagado, no lo curan
médicos ni boticarios.

Proverb

Mal vecino es el amor,
y do no lo hay es peor.

Proverb

Esta fuerza tiene el amor, si es perfecto:
que olvidamos nuestro contento
por contentar a quien amamos.

Santa Teresa de Jesús

Que sólo amor es el que da valor a todas las cosas.

Santa Teresa de Jesús

El amor jamás está ocioso.

Santa Teresa de Jesús

...presente ante mis ojos la imagino,
y lleno de humildad y amor la adoro.

Fray Luis de León

A wounded heart is not cured
by doctors or pharmacists.

Love is a bad neighbour,
but to have none is worse.

This power has love, if it is perfect:
it makes us forget our own happiness
to make happy the one we love.

It is love alone that gives worth to all things.

Love is never lazy.

... here before my eyes, I see her sweet guise,
and with humbleness and love I worship her.

Los yerros por amores dignos son de perdonar.

Proverb

Querer a quien no me quiere,
mal haya quien tal hiciere.

Proverb

Y donde no hay amor, ponga amor,
y sacarás amor.

San Juan de la Cruz

El alma enamorada es alma blanda, mansa,
humilde y paciente.

San Juan de la Cruz

El alma que anda en amor, ni
cansa ni se cansa.

San Juan de la Cruz

Amado mío, todo lo áspero y trabajoso
quiero para mí y todo lo suave
y sabroso quiero para ti.

San Juan de la Cruz

Mistakes made for love are worthy of forgiveness.

To love someone who loves you not
is a curse on one begot.

Where love does not exist, plant it
and it will grow.

A heart in love is tender, gentle,
humble and patient.

The soul that walks in love is neither
wearisome nor wearies.

Beloved, all that is harsh and difficult
I want for myself and all that is gentle
and sweet for thee.

Más tira mujer que soga.

Proverb

La mujer y el vino sacan al hombre de tino.

Proverb

¡Oh llama de amor viva
que tiernamente hieres
a mi alma en el más profundo centro!

San Juan de la Cruz

¿Dónde estás, señora mía,
que no te duele mi mal?
O no lo sabes, señora,
o eres falsa y desleal.

Miguel de Cervantes

La razón de la sinrazón que a mi razón se hace,
de tal manera mi razón enflaquece,
que con razón me quejo de la vuestra fermosura.

Miguel de Cervantes

A woman pulls more than a rope.

Women and wine drive men out of their mind.

Oh ardent flame of love
that wounds so tenderly,
scorching the deepest regions of my heart!

Oh, where art thou, sweet lady mine,
that thou dost not feel this my pain?
Knowest thou not, or, lady fair,
dost thou truth and loyalty feign?

The reason for the unreasonableness with which
you treat my reason, so impairs my reason,
that with reason I complain of your beauty.

El amor es ciego.

Proverb

A la prueba, buen amor.

Proverb

Plégaos, señora, de membraros deste vuestro sujeto corazón,
que tantas cuitas por vuestro amor padece.

Miguel de Cervantes

Que nunca fue desdichado
amor que fue conocido.

Miguel de Cervantes

Ella pelea en mí y vence en mí, y yo vivo
y respiro en ella, y tengo vida y ser.

Miguel de Cervantes

No es lo mismo el amor que el apetito,
que en diferente parte se aposenta:
La virtud al primero lo alimenta,
al segundo aliméntalo el delito.

Lupercio L. de Argensola

Love is blind.

True love must be proved.

Deign, dearest lady, to think on your captive heart,
which for love of you endures such pain.

One could ne'er call ill-fated
a love that is requited.

She fights and vanquishes in me, and I live
and breathe in her, and I have life and being.

Love is not the same as desire, for they
live in different dwellings:
Virtue nourishes the first, while
the second is nourished by vice.

A quien quiero no me quiere,
y a quien me quiere no quiero.

Proverb

Donde hay querer, todo se hace bien.

Proverb

Déjame en paz, Amor tirano,
déjame en paz.

Luis de Góngora

No sabe qué es amor quien no te ama.

Lope de Vega

Del amor el fuego
y del tiempo el frío,
al dulce amor mío
quitan el sosiego.

Lope de Vega

Armonía es puro amor,
porque el amor es concierto.

Lope de Vega

I love who loves me not,
and who loves me, I love not.

Where there is love, all things are done well.

Leave me in peace, tyrant Love,
leave me in peace.

He knows nothing of love who loves not thee.

The fire of love
and the cold of time,
deprive my sweet love
of his peace of mind.

Harmony is pure love,
for love is a concerto.

Advertid que amor es sordo,
y que no escucha palabras
el día que está en su trono.

Lope de Vega

Sin amor no se pudiera ni aun el mundo conservar.

Lope de Vega

Amor es rey que iguala con justa ley
la seda con el sayal.

Tirso de Molina

Querránte bien si regalas,
y más si regalas más.

Francisco de Trillo y Figueroa

Este amoroso tormento
que en mi corazón se ve,
sé que lo siento, y no sé
la causa por qué lo siento.

Sor Juana Inés de la Cruz

Beware, love is deaf as a stone,
and will listen not to words
the day he sits on the throne.

Without love the world itself would not survive.

Love is a king that, with just law,
rends alike silk and sackcloth.

They will love you dearly if you give them presents,
and better if you give them more.

This strange torment of love
that in my heart doth vie,
I know that I feel it,
but alas, know not why.

Amor de monja, fuego de estopas.
Proverb

La zagala y el garzón,
para en uno son.
Proverb

Es el amor que al mismo amor adora.
José de Espronceda

Otro cielo el amor te prometía.
José de Espronceda

Brota en el cielo del amor la fuente
que a fecundar el universo mana.
José de Espronceda

El alma que hablar puede con los ojos,
también puede besar con la mirada.
Gustavo Adolfo Bécquer

A nun's love is a raging inferno.

The youth and the maid,
for each other are made.

Love adores being in love.

Another heaven love did promise you.

The fount of love has its well-spring in heaven,
whence it flows to fecundate the world.

The soul that can speak with the eyes,
can also kiss with a gaze.

Afortunado en el juego, desafortunado en amores.

Proverb

Quien bien te quiere, bien te sueña.

Proverb

Como yo te he querido... desengáñate,
nadie así te amará.

Gustavo Adolfo Bécquer

Yo creo que si me muriera y fueras a
pasear junto a mi sepultura, desde lo hondo de la
tierra sentiría tus pasos.

Benito Pérez Galdós

Temblaba en los brazos varoniles como la
paloma en las garras del águila.

Benito Pérez Galdós

¡El amor!, ¡siempre el amor atravesándose
en el sendero de las grandes empresas!,
¡qué de tiempo le ha hecho perder a la humanidad
el dichoso amor!

Miguel de Unamuno

Lucky at cards, unlucky in love.

He who loves you a lot, dreams of you a lot.

As I have loved you... be not deceived,
no-one will ever love you so.

I believe that if I should die, and you were to
walk near my grave, from the very depths of the
earth I would hear your footsteps.

She trembled in his manly arms
like the dove in the eagle's claws.

Love! love always getting in the way
of great deeds! How much time has humanity
lost for love's blessed sake!

La quiero por inercia, por hábito;
soy una víctima del amor.

Miguel de Unamuno

No haremos con la pedagogía
genios mientras no se elimine el amor.

Miguel de Unamuno

El amor pasajero tiene el encanto breve,
y ofrece un igual término para el gozo y la pena.

Rubén Darío

Renaceré yo piedra
y aún te amaré mujer a ti.

Juan Ramón Jiménez

¡En vano es que no quieras!

Juan Ramón Jiménez

¡Eres eterno, amor,
como la primavera!

Juan Ramón Jiménez

I love her out of inertia, out of habit;
I am a victim of love.

We shall not create geniuses through pedagogy
until we have eliminated love.

Ephemeral love holds a brief enchantment,
and offers the same end for joy and sorrow.

Were I reborn a stone,
woman, I would love thee still.

In vain is your not loving!

Love, you are eternal
like springtime.

All translations by Juan and Susan Serrano, editors, except the following:

Love	Henry W. Longfellow
Praise of Little Women	" "
Macias' Song	Jeremiah H. Wiffen
Thy face is written in my soul	" "
Nemoroso (from Eclogue I)	" "
I cannot cease to love	John Bowring
Woman's Jealousy	" "
Pure Spirit	Henry W. Longfellow
Love	Charles Jarvis
Love's hapless mariner	" "
What causes all my grief and pain?	" "
Faint Heart Never Won Fair Lady	John Bowring
Amaryllis	" "
Love, love	Percy Bysshe Shelley